FIRST 15 LESSONS

PIANO

by Barbara Henry

Includes Audio & Video Access

PLAYBACK+
Speed • Pitch • Balance • Loop

To access audio, video, and extra content visit:
www.halleonard.com/mylibrary

Enter Code
2204-4064-2484-8482

ISBN 978-1-5400-1247-0

HAL•LEONARD®
7777 W. BLUEMOUND RD. P.O. BOX 13819 MILWAUKEE, WI 53213

Visit Hal Leonard Online at
www.halleonard.com

The Piano Keyboard

A full piano keyboard consists of 88 white and black keys. Some digital or electronic keyboards may have fewer than 88. The black keys alternate in groups of two and three. If you play the keys to the right you are moving **up** the keyboard and sound higher. If you play the keys to the left you are moving **down** and sound lower.

1A

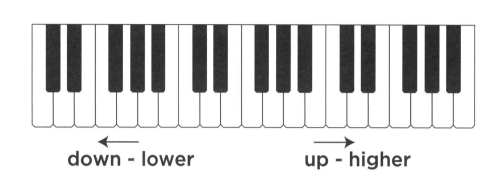

← down - lower   up - higher →

1B

Sit squarely at the keyboard with a straight back; arms hanging loosely from shoulders. The bench or chair should be high enough for elbows to be slightly higher than the keyboard. When playing the piano, numbers are assigned to each finger.

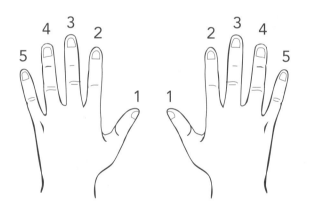

1C

The first seven letters of the alphabet are used to name the keys on the piano.

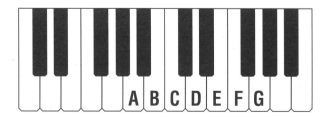

A B C D E F G

Learning the pitches C, D and E

Use the groups of two black keys to learn C-D-E. Play all the C-D-E groups on your keyboard. For right hand, place finger 2 on C, finger 3 on D and finger 4 on E. For left hand, place finger 4 on C, finger 3 on D and finger 2 on E.

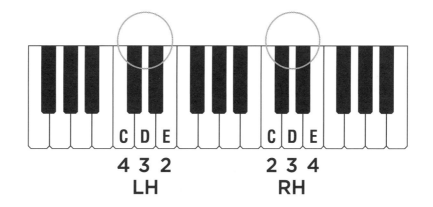

It's possible to use different finger combinations when playing the piano. Try playing C-D-E with right hand using fingers 1-2-3. Play left hand using fingers 3-2-1.

Learning the pitches F, G, A and B

Use the groups of three black keys to learn the letter names of the remaining white keys. Play right-hand thumb on F, 2 on G, 3 on A, and 4 on B. Play left-hand finger 4 on F, 3 on G, 2 on A, and thumb on B.

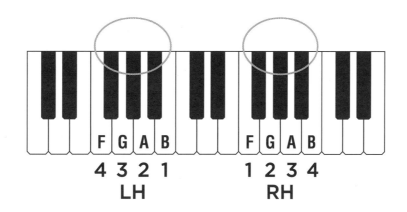

When playing, keep fingers curved and the knuckles rounded, not flat. A rounded hand position allows the fingers to move more freely. Imagine gently cupping your hand around a tennis ball.

Rhythm

Music is written using symbols called **notes**. Each type of note has a specific rhythmic value.

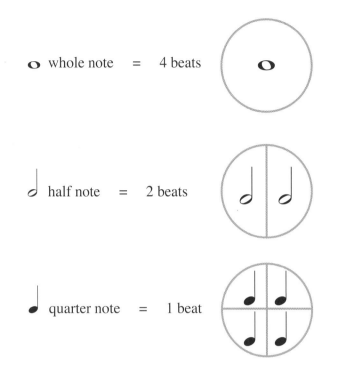

o whole note = 4 beats

♩ half note = 2 beats

♩ quarter note = 1 beat

Combining note values creates **rhythm**. A continuous pulse is called a **beat**. Beats are grouped into **measures** using bar lines. A **double bar line** marks the end of the song. **Tempo** indicates the speed of the beat.

 2A
Clap the rhythm below.

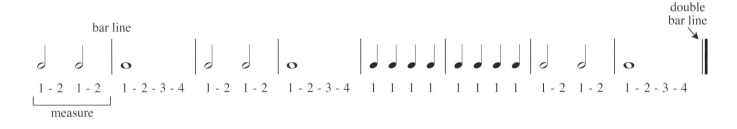

Play "Hot Cross Buns" on page 5 using a three black key group. Use the finger numbers given for right hand. Try it again with the left hand. Notice that when playing left hand the first note is played with finger 2 instead of finger 4.

Hot Cross Buns

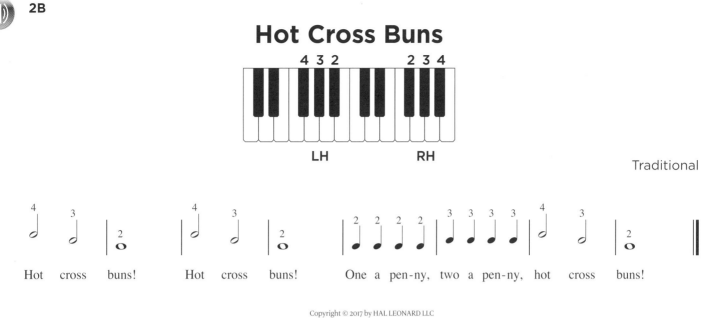

Traditional

Hot cross buns!   Hot cross buns!   One a pen-ny, two a pen-ny, hot cross buns!

Before playing "The Moon Is Coming Out," clap the rhythm. Count the beats of each note as you clap. Play this song using a two black key group for right hand and a three black key group for left hand.

The Moon Is Coming Out (Tzuki)
(from CHILDREN'S SONGS FROM JAPAN)

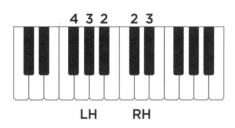

Words and Music by Akiyama Kazue and Florence White

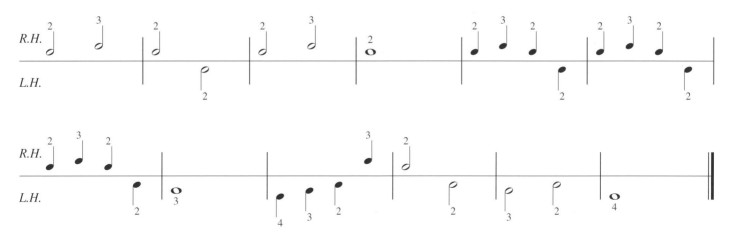

Reading Music

Notes are written on a **staff**; five horizontal lines and four spaces. Placement of the notes determines the **pitch**, how high or low a note sounds. The higher the note on the staff, the higher the pitch. The lower the note on the staff, the lower the pitch.

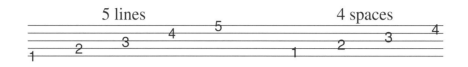

A **clef** determines the names of the notes on the lines and spaces. **Treble clef**, also known as **G clef**, names the second line G, the G above middle C. Right hand usually plays in treble clef.

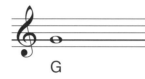

Below, "Hot Cross Buns" is written in treble clef. Note the names of the white keys you'll play as well as the finger numbers needed.

3A

Hot Cross Buns

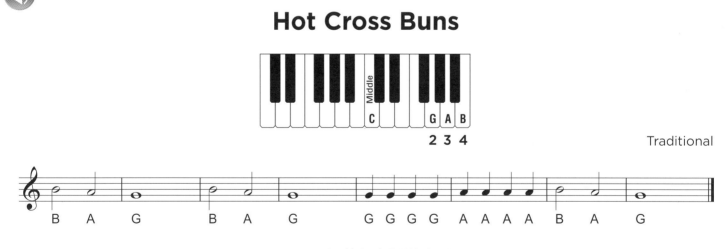

Bass clef, also known as **F clef**, names the fourth line F, the F below middle C. Left hand usually plays in bass clef.

F

"Hot Cross Buns" can be played using different white keys, but the same pattern of notes that move up, down, and repeat. This time play "Hot Cross Buns" in bass clef with left hand.

3B

Hot Cross Buns

Traditional

When notes move from one key to the next key (line to a space, or space to a line on the staff), it's often described as a **step**. Notes that skip a key (line to line, or space to space) can be described as a **skip**. Notice the steps and skip labeled in the song below. "Au Clair de la Lune" begins with three repeated G notes.

3C

Au Clair De La Lune

French Folk Song

3D

Go online for more practice identifying steps and skips.

Rests and Eighth Notes

In music, sound and silence are equally important. For every note value of sound there is a symbol that equals the same amount of silence. These symbols are called **rests**.

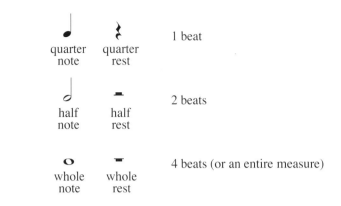

Clap and count the rhythms below. Each measure contains at least one rest.

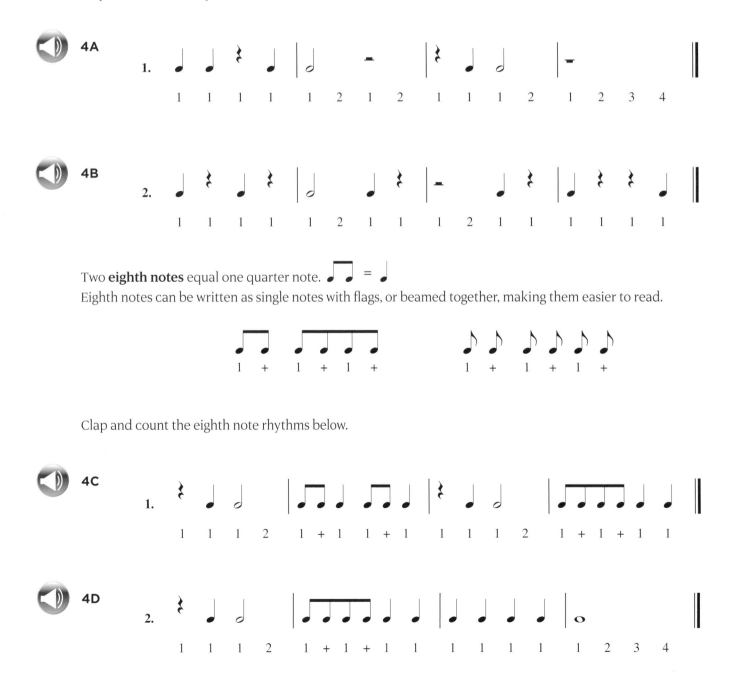

Two **eighth notes** equal one quarter note.

Eighth notes can be written as single notes with flags, or beamed together, making them easier to read.

Clap and count the eighth note rhythms below.

"Good News" is written in treble clef using a three note pattern and quarter rests. Clap and count the rhythm before playing the song on the piano. Do not clap on the rest.

4E

Good News
(treble clef-right hand)

Traditional Spiritual

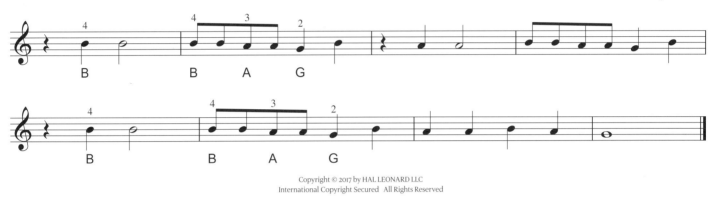

Now play "Good News" written in bass clef. This time left hand starts on B with finger 2.

4F

Good News
(bass clef-left hand)

Traditional Spiritual

Five-Finger Patterns

"Little River Flowing" uses a **C five-finger pattern.** The notes step up and down, one note to the next. This song is written in bass clef. Start on C with left hand. **Finger Numbers** indicate which fingers to use.

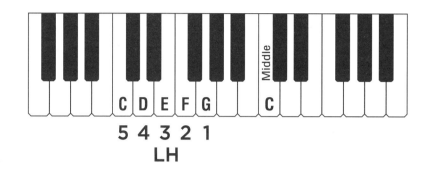

 5A

Little River Flowing
(Using C Five-Finger Pattern)

Folk Melody

Now play "Little River Flowing" using a **G five finger pattern**. Play treble clef with right hand.

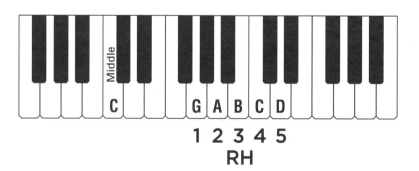

5B

Little River Flowing
(Using G Five-Finger Pattern)

Folk Melody

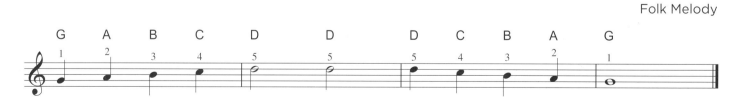

"Skipping" uses a C five-finger pattern, but instead of moving from one note to the next note, the notes "skip" from one to another. Notice that notes that move from a line to another line "skip" the space in between. Notes that move from a space to another space "skip" the line in between.

5C

Skipping
(Using C Five-Finger Pattern)

Play "Skipping" using a G five-finger pattern. Start with right-hand finger 1 on G.

5D

Skipping
(Using G Five-Finger Pattern)

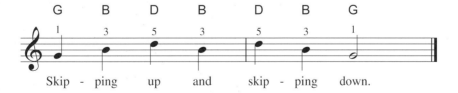

The Grand Staff

Piano music is written on an upper and lower staff joined together, called the **Grand Staff.**

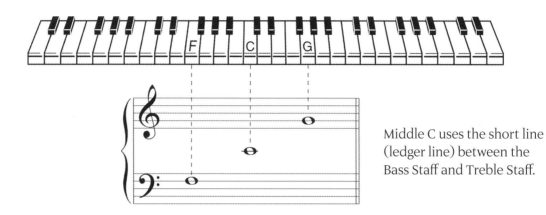

Middle C uses the short line (ledger line) between the Bass Staff and Treble Staff.

The two staves are joined together using a bar line and a brace to form the **Grand Staff**. The higher staff has a symbol at the beginning called the **Treble clef**. It shows the notes that are played on **Middle C** and higher. Notice that the treble clef circles the second line on the staff. This is the G line, which is five notes above middle C. The lower staff has a symbol at the beginning of it called the **Bass clef**. It shows the notes that are played on **Middle C** and lower. Notice that the clef starts on the fourth line and has a dot placed above and below the fourth line. The fourth line is Bass F. **Treble G, Middle C** and **Bass F** are three notes that can be used as reference points to help you to identify which notes to play.

6A

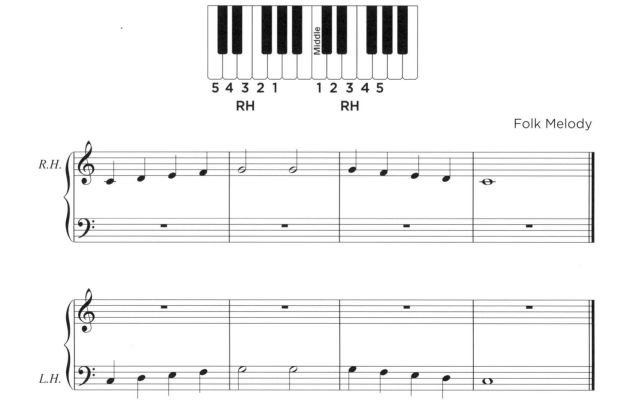

Little River Flowing

Folk Melody

Practice naming the notes on the grand staff below. Play the notes after you identify them. Check your work online.*

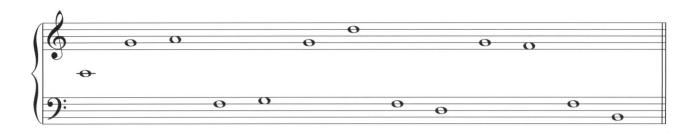

A **Time Signature** appears at the beginning of every piece of music. It has two numbers. The top number indicates the number of beats per measure. The bottom number represents what kind of note will equal one beat.

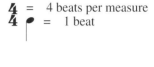

Play "Skipping" on the grand staff. Notice the skips moving from line to line in the right hand, and space to space in the left hand.

6B

Skipping

5 4 3 2 1   1 2 3 4 5
RH   RH

6C

* See the grand staff chart online. Use this chart as a reference as needed.

LESSON 7

Dotted Notes and Ties

A **dot** placed after a note increases the value of the note by half. For example, a dotted half note equals three beats.

$\downarrow$ + $\cdot$ = 3 beats

$\downarrow\cdot$ = dotted half note

Note the time signature in the German folk song "Listen to the Wind." There are three beats per measure, and the quarter note equals one beat. **Dotted half notes** equal three beats.

7A

Listen to the Wind

German Folk Song

A **tie** is used to lengthen the value of a note, often beyond a barline. In measure 7 of "Barcarolle" the B is **tied** over the bar into the next measure. Now the B will last for six beats. Play the first B, and hold the note for the value of both dotted half notes "tied" together.

7B

Barcarolle
from THE TALES OF HOFFMANN (LES CONTES D'HOFFMANN)

By Jacques Offenbach

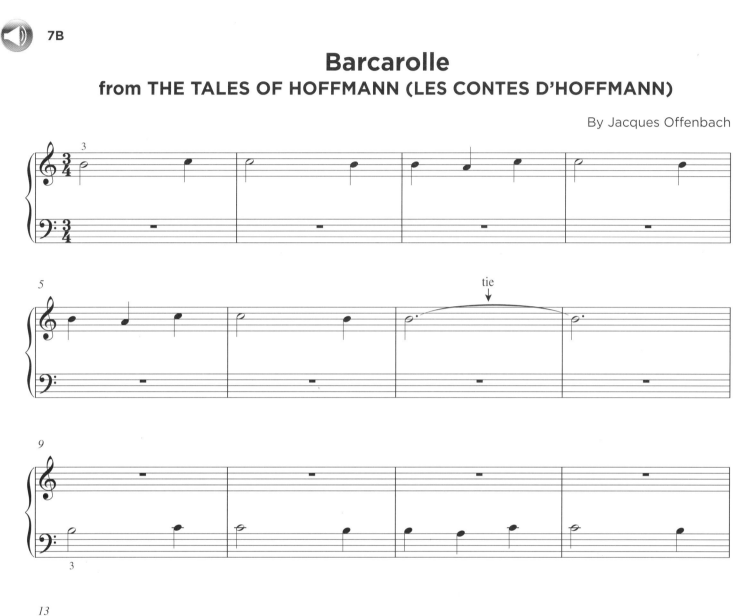

LESSON 8

Playing Melodies

The folk song "Aura Lee" was made popular by '50s Rock 'n' Roll icon Elvis Presley as "Love Me Tender." The melody is centered around middle C, and passes from left hand to right hand throughout. Start with both thumbs sharing middle C. Play middle C with left hand when the C is written in the bass clef. Use right hand when middle C is written in the treble clef.

Love Me Tender

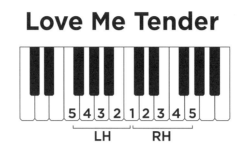

Words and Music by Elvis Presley and Vera Matson

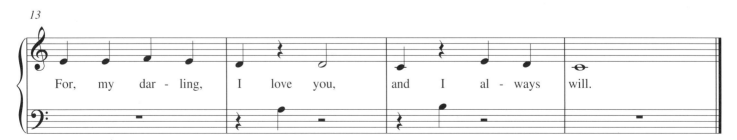

Dynamics determine volume. Symbols using Italian words represent the varying degrees of sound.

p	mp	mf	f
piano	*mezzo piano*	*mezzo forte*	*forte*
soft	medium soft	medium loud	loud

Note the dynamic change in "Bluebird, Bluebird."

8A

Bluebird, Bluebird

American Nursery Rhyme

Increase your note-reading skill. Name the notes on the grand staff.

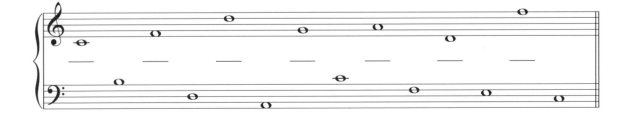

8B

Go online to check your answers and find more practice exercises.

Sharps and Flats

A **sharp sign** [♯] in front of a note **raises** the note a **half step**. When you see a sharped note, play the next key to the **right**, black or white.

9A

Au Clair De La Lune

French Folk Song

A **flat sign** [♭] in front of a note **lowers** the note a half step. When a note is flat, play the next key to the **left**, black or white.

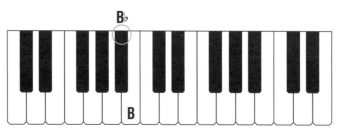

Love Somebody

Traditional

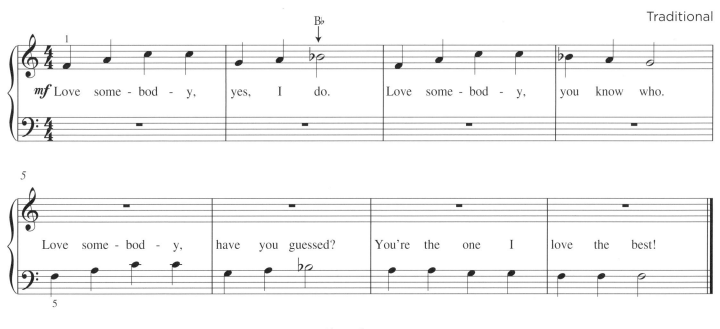

Sharps and flats within a measure can be called **accidentals**. An accidental alters that note for the entire measure. The bar line cancels the sharp or flat.

Silver Moon Boat

Chinese Folk Song

Playing Hands Together

Take a look at lines one and three of the classical melody "To a Wild Rose." Learn the left-hand measures first, taking care to hold the whole notes for the full measure when you add the right hand. The **fermata** sign ⌢ in the last measure means to hold the notes for longer than the written value. A **tempo head** above the time signature indicates the speed or character of a song.

10A

To a Wild Rose
from WOODLAND SKETCHES, OP. 51, NO. 1

By Edward MacDowell

"Chiapanecas" divides the melody between your hands, with hands playing together at the end of each line. Study the hands together measures. Right hand moves down by a step: left hand plays repeated notes. Practice these measures alone if they are challenging to play at first.

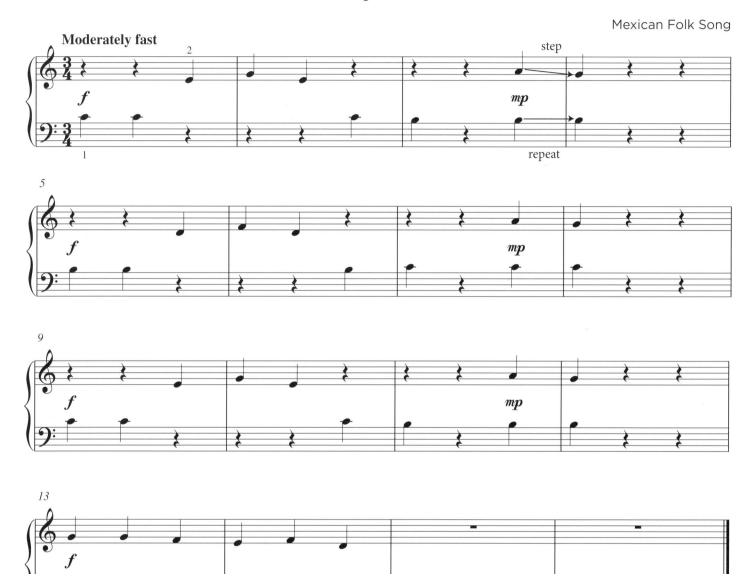

10B

Chiapanecas

Mexican Folk Song

Dotted Quarter Notes and Repeat Signs

When a dot is placed after a note, it increases the value of that note by half. For example, a dotted half note equals three beats. And so, a **dotted quarter note** receives 1 and ½ beats. Often, an eighth note follows a dotted quarter note, and together the two notes equal two full beats.

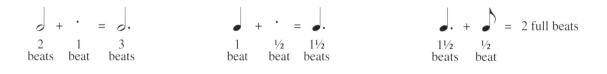

Compare the rhythms below. They sound the same but are notated differently. This illustrates how the dot takes the place of the tied eighth note in the second beat of the measure.

11A

1 + 2 + 3 4   1 + 2 + 3 4

Repeat signs indicate a section of the music will be repeated.

repeat sign
(play again)

First and Second Ending brackets direct you to repeat as indicated, then continue to the second ending. The first time through, play the measure under the first ending bracket. On the repeat, skip the first bracket and continue with the measure under the second bracket.

11B

There are two dotted quarter note rhythms in "My Heart Will Go On." Listen to the online audio if you are unfamiliar with this song, and sing along as you play the dotted rhythms.

1 + 2 + 3 4   1 2 3 + 4 +

My Heart Will Go On
(Love Theme from 'Titanic')
from the Paramount and Twentieth Century Fox Motion Picture TITANIC

Music by James Horner
Lyric by Will Jennings

repeat from measure 1

repeat from measure 9

LESSON 12

Sixteenth Notes

Two 16th notes equal one eighth note:

Count and clap the example below.

12A

12B

Blackbird

Words and Music by John Lennon and Paul McCartney

Swing is a term used in jazz. To "swing" eighth notes, play them in an unequal pattern of long and short eighths. Eighth notes **on** the beat are long, eighth notes **off** the beat (on the "and") are short. When (♪♪ = ♪♪) is next to the tempo, it indicates swing eighths.

Count and clap the example below, using swing eighths.*

12C

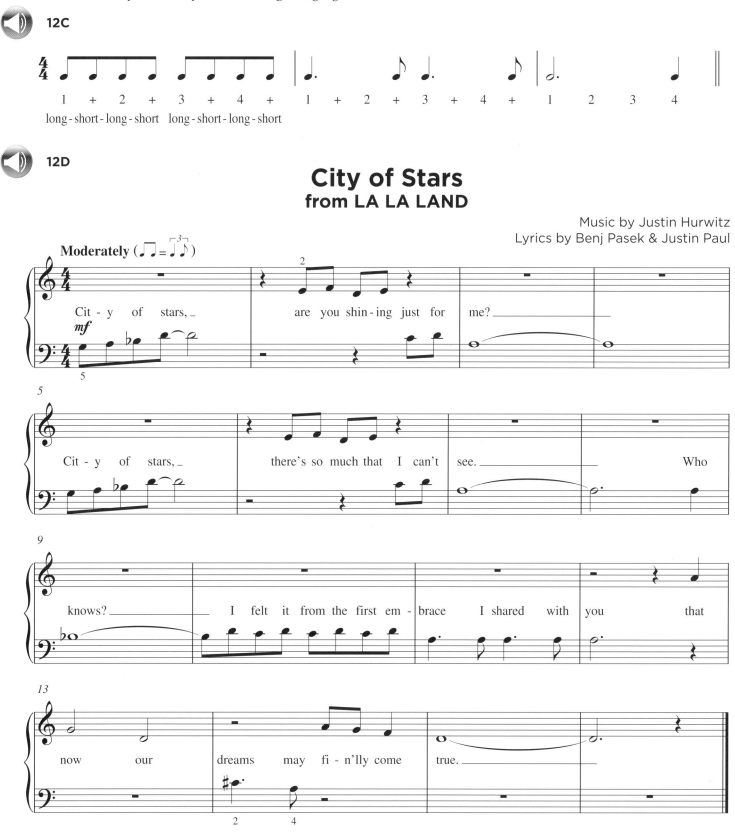

City of Stars
from LA LA LAND

Music by Justin Hurwitz
Lyrics by Benj Pasek & Justin Paul

12D

© 2016 Justin Hurwitz Music (BMI), B Lion Music (BMI), and Warner-Tamerlane Publishing Corp. (BMI), all administered by Warner-Tamerlane Publishing Corp. (BMI)/Pick In A Pinch Music (ASCAP), breathelike music (ASCAP), A Lion Music (ASCAP), and WB Music Corp. (ASCAP), all administered by WB Music Corp. (ASCAP)
All Rights Reserved Used by Permission

*Use the bonus online metronome to help you play the swing eighths. As you continue through the lessons, practice with the metronome at a slow tempo first, increasing the tempo as you become more comfortable with a steady beat.

Left-Hand Accompaniment

Accompaniment refers to the musical material that supports the melody. In piano music the left hand usually plays the accompaniment. There are various accompaniment patterns, such as alternating notes, single notes, and various chord patterns.

The classical melody "Spring" from Vivaldi's *Four Seasons* uses an alternating note pattern in the left hand. It begins with an **upbeat**, a note (or notes) that come before the first full measure.

🔊 13

Spring
from THE FOUR SEASONS

By Antonio Vivaldi

"Lavender Blue" uses a single-note accompaniment, and contains **finger stretches** in both hands. This allows the hand position to span more notes as you extend your fingers.

Lavender Blue (Dilly Dilly)
from SO DEAR TO MY HEART

Words by Larry Morey
Music by Eliot Daniel

"The Girl from Ipanema" uses a **chordal** accompaniment. **Chords** are groups of two or more notes played at the same time.

The Girl From Ipanema (Garôta De Ipanema)

Music by Antonio Carlos Jobim
English Words by Norman Gimbel
Original Words by Vinicius De Moraes

LESSON 14

Hand Shifts

A **hand shift** is simply picking the hand up and moving it to another place on the keyboard. In "Piano Man" the left hand stays in one place for the entire song. The right hand moves in measure 17, and then moves again in measure 26, right before the D.C. al Fine (measure 28). **D.C. al Fine** is a direction to return to the beginning of the song (**D.C.**) and play until **Fine** (the "end").

14

Piano Man

Words and Music by Billy Joel

In "Linus and Lucy" the right hand stays in one position throughout, but the left hand contains finger stretches and hand shifts. Practice moving from left-hand finger 5 on C in the first measure to finger 5 on the black key, E♭ (measure 7), and follow all other fingering given. **D.C. al Coda** means to return to the beginning of the song, play until "To Coda" and then skip to the measures marked "Coda."

Linus and Lucy

By Vince Guaraldi

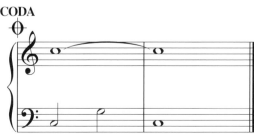

Shifts in Both Hands

As you continue to learn new songs you'll increase the range of keyboard used, rarely staying in one place for an entire song, or even an entire section. At first this can seem challenging, but careful practice and attention to fingering and shifts will help you be successful.

The 2016 pop hit "Handclap" performed originally by the group Fitz and the Tantrums has a lot of repeated notes in the melody. Anchor right hand on A until measure 10, then move finger 3 up a skip to C. That's where your right hand will stay for the rest of the song.

Left hand has an interesting bass line that begins with finger 5 on low A. Shift left hand in measure 10, Moving finger 3 down to low G. Learn this song in sections, practicing each hand alone as needed.

15

HandClap

Words and Music by Eric Frederic, Samuel Hollander, Michael Fitzpatrick,
Joseph Karnes, James King, Jeremy Ruzumna, Noelle Scaggs and John Wicks

I can make your hands clap. Ev - er - y night___ when the stars come out,
ing 'til the sun comes out___

___ am I the on - ly liv - ing soul a - round? ___ Need to be - lieve___
___ and when we wake___ we'd be the on - ly sound. ___ Get on my knees___

1.
___ you could hold me down ___ 'cause I'm in need ___ of some - thing good right
___ and say a prayer, James

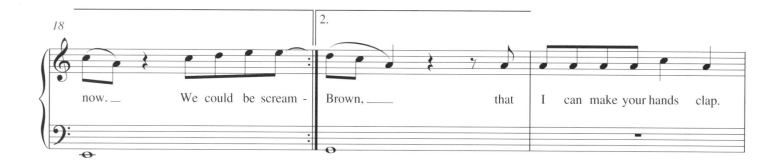

2.
now. ___ We could be scream - Brown, ___ that I can make your hands clap.

Learn each hand separately as you begin to work on "Ticket to the Moon." The first right hand finger stretch may look tricky, but it's very easy. Start with thumb on E and stretch finger 3 to A. Once you're on A stay in this position until measure 9, reaching down with right-hand thumb to play E when necessary. For these first eight measures, left hand stays in one position. At measure 9, both hands move: right-hand thumb up to A, and left-hand thumb down to A.

Ticket to the Moon

Words and Music by Jeff Lynne